Three Hands None

Three Hands None

Denise Bergman

Black Lawrence Press

Black
Lawrence
Press

www.blacklawrence.com

Executive Editor: Diane Goettel
Book Design: Amy Freels
Cover Design: Zoe Norvell

Copyright © Denise Bergman 2019
ISBN: 978-1-62557-709-2

Published 2019 by Black Lawrence Press.
Printed in the United States.

For Esther

Table of Contents

he had three hands I had none

where were my hands where were they

under the cotton sheet

his three loud hands shouted precise non-negotiable commands

his knife-blade hand. his hot blinding-flashlight hand. his granite-weight hand crushing my lips against gums and teeth

his hands stuttered filth in the eloquent language of power

look at hands

in uniform salute. waving from chandeliered balconies over town plazas. tossing benedictions. pushing round red buttons behind closed oak doors. pulling round red triggers. throwing darts at paper wall maps

manicured fingers snapping. snap snap snap

he knew my eyelashes. the Clearasil dot on my cheek. the
rhythm my nostrils bellow in unchecked sleep. my lower lip's
tremor

he knew in a split-second what a lover takes months to see

he knew my Adam's apple's shallow throb and my throat's
spasm at the touch of the blade

his say it *his blade*

from the outside it sounded like what it looked like. barks
then screams. barks screams then a door's nasty creak. it
looked like desperation's aftermath. it was aftermath. he fled.
there was no one but me. the dog panting and me

in the belly of night where was I. I had simply gone to sleep
with an inch of May breeze

from the outside barks screams pounding silence. someone
called the police I called the police 911 police

then catch-as-catch-can men went to bed with baseball bats
and women kept bulbs burning

I fought back by waiting

the chokehold of time stretched compressed stretched
compressed. a rapidly fraying rubber band

crickets swore off middle-of-the-night jabber. common
grackle singsong drowned in swelter

his rasping voice on his whitewater breath crashed against
my face

his voice deep inside my ears

photos of men was it this one that. I tell them I hadn't seen his face the flashlight melted my eyes

mug shots again was it this one that. I hadn't seen hadn't seen

did I smell his breath his underarm stench his filtered or filterless. did he smell me

he watched me. he locked my face naked in detention

he knew who I was knew me when I crossed the street knows who I am knows this is me

knows me. in the grocery aisle he sees me stripped to less than essence

he held me down. the heft of his hand the precise edge of his blade squeezed me pierced me emptied me of substance

I am not playing here with agency

this is what powerless is

barebones nothing

barebones and muscleless. skeleton collapsed

lunch became bread and water

motion was turning my head to look at the door

watch the door

thought was imploded chaos. speech was a pageless lexicon

sleep was a useless plan. exhaustion buzzed like a swinging hive

my home my skin locked me out

breakfast was a sip of juice

supper was bread and water. the week after, a fruit

what now

I waited. tea teacup teapot

rubbing the dog's forehead when it let me

sleeping noon to three up all night

the apartment bright as a penny arcade

dull or acute my choice and I chose
depending on the day

as I had chosen to obey
his blade

silence rings through the arcade

when after I leave I stay

alone
with the wary dog who can't wait
to be rid of me

home is skin but I couldn't inhabit my skin

empty limbs empty head empty pelvis bowl. pockets behind
scapulas. cage around liver and lung. ringing in my ears
drained down my hollow tube neck

no one inhabited my skin a vicious biting no one inhabited my
skin

airtight insulated pores nothing seeped in leaked out

inside me the hard shrunken kernel of what I had been rattled
like a single shriveled bean in a hand-painted maraca

shake (delay) move (delay) sound

the way I remember the end of the beginning the dog barked
the man lost his hold then I screamed

or after he fled I screamed

did he release his hand from my mouth or his knife from my
throat

when his hand pressed my mouth his knife was where

did he fling the knife onto the bed to empty his hand to press
on my mouth and still keep the flashlight's beam blinding

or did he remove his hand to grab the knife

redundant a knife at my throat a hand pressed over my mouth.
sores and bleeding lip and gums did he say I have a knife don't
scream did he say I have a knife I will kill you if you scream

I thought he has a knife he will kill me if I move he will kill me
finally the dog barked

and from me a defiant don't-scream scream an obedient-to-
self withheld scream I screamed after the dog barked the man
fled did I call the police who called

told again and again the story becomes its own citation

its own list of definitions

I stared at my knees in the mirror. lifted one shoulder in a half-shrug. raised a hand. twisted at the waist. saw that I am

saw the door behind me

walked into the living room touched a chair book plant. saw that they were. dared touch the doorknob. dared wipe the 911 fingerprints off the phone

opened the window and listened. outside where I lived and didn't live a woman sang. in a city in a building in a room if nowhere else in a body once her own

the next day was all days from then on and the dog what could
I do to undo what I did and hadn't done

the dog averted its eyes from my eyes moved from where I
stood or sat and watched out for itself without me

its red leash clipped to the handsome red collar pulled
taut. our six feet clicked and tapped on the sidewalk an
unsynchronized rhythm

a week later when a man pants down knocked on the
apartment door I fled down the back alley alone. understand
I tried to take the dog it jumped from my arms ran from the
room the dog that saved my life wanted only to hide from me

white-diamond chest long straight whiskers folded-kerchief
ear wrinkle brow a mole on the left jowl. I sat on the floor and
watched it sleep. if an animal can wish this one wished it had
never met me

the pod covering the kernel that is all that is left of me shrivels
and peels away. the kernel falls to the floor rolls under the
table sofa refrigerator rug after a bath rolls under the tub

rolls and disappears. the kernel who I am is mottled pits ridges
scars. an ordinary lookalike kernel. an energy depleted kernel.
the young woman sleeps for weeks

she sleeps I sleep for weeks a waking sleep though I can't sleep
can't fall or stay asleep

on hands and knees I retrieve the kernel lock it in my fist still I
don't sleep

sleep is waking

waking is remembering

I said to no one stop stop what you're doing

listen

I was busy full-time searching for me

never begged asked you or you

I was a footnote in an ancient volume's chapter

same old story

I asked no one to stop. listen. I was locked in a soundproof
looks-like-me skin

I was locked out of the skin scrambling to get in

at times I was the skin

in dreams I straddled an enormous orb that split like a sluggish
amoeba. which side would I ride

which side would I relinquish

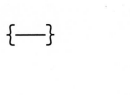

he knows who I am

each man I pass on the way to work
knows who I am

on the sweltering bus in the corner cafe in line at the bank

why me
who was I to him who was I

how many days weeks or spontaneously once
did he follow me

was I a fixation a woman who went to bed naked

or was I a random no one

a no one

believe me he didn't know a dog slept at my feet

did it end for him when he ended it

or was he the man at the door a week later
pants down cock in his hand

word on the street she still lives there
she hasn't moved out yet

he knows who I am he sees parts of me I don't see. the back
of my back the top of my head. in his surveillant camera
eye whim he shoots me. from a corner lamppost video. as a
shadow pickpocket working the crowd

he takes snapshots of my chickenscratch words on paper
scraps. letters and bills he microfiches before the postman
drops my mail in the box after my name unseals in my hand

he knows he sees me he knows me he sees me and collects
and files his data. my every gesture procured in stealth. with
whom does he confide divide interpret his shares of conquest

cloaked he trails my patter *he he he* trails me until the
morsels and paces I talk and walk are sounded and shaped for
his gleaning

he gleans gathers and from the remains of *the remains of* he
shapes a whole he assumes is the whole

I know what I don't see. he is here and here and I have become
the girl who swallows her gum before the teacher enters the
classroom. the girl who doesn't startle when her premature
bra is snapped. the woman who concedes her thoughts to no
one and buries cognition in impenetrable depths

he he he gleaned me. what's left are leafless stalks too thin to
catch a wind

tattered and tight when did I expose again my skin to light.
kitchen fluorescent hallway incandescent. hazy St. Louis sun

I sweated inside matted wool terror filthy as a sheep

sweated even under a flowered cotton sheet

shed layers wool cotton skin to where what-is-left lives when
all is peeled away

naked and when the spinning slowed a toe stepped
tentatively out. a scout

on a bike with broken brakes you skip skip skip your foot to
stop. risk a twisted ankle

a twisted ankle's no distraction from a mouth with oozing
sores a neck stiff in pain

my mouth my neck I must say that word: *my*

I can write pages but when I write *my* I cry

I can write but when I write *my* I cry. odd strange I've told this
story a thousand times it is me telling it me it is about me me I
write *my* and I cry

a twenty-year-old woman alone in a tiny speck of bed deep
inside sleep wakes up to a man with a knife at her throat. *my*

is the distance the knife traveled to slash the kernel of her being into pieces

my is the nanosecond minute lifetime. *my* is eternity's heft. he leaned on my chest his elbow in my rib one hand over my mouth

his three hands one on my mouth one with the knife one holding the flashlight so close my eyes were on fire

the dog had one upright ear and one without spine a kerchief
folded in half. a white diamond on its black chest and one
white paw. the dog that saved me was a pup. runt of the litter
my neighbor said placing its warm belly on my shoulder. take
it it just lags behind

it trusted me before it didn't trust me after. it trusted me
before is a question

what did this do to the puppy ignored by siblings and pushed
from its mother's teat. my quiet home soft bed curled-up
sleep then a man smashes its leg-twitching dream. a friend
says start with the dog so let's start

the dog was a blend of a this and a that and soon a before and
an after

I named it Yarrow for the I Ching sticks cast to decipher
choices

our first day I whispered into the folded ear *let's take a walk*
and my puppy noticed

the dog was my dog

my life was saved by my dog

a friend tosses in "compassion" "society" "circumstances." I
tell her I don't care

I don't care

born into a tangled skein of back-stabbing brothers. so what.
wrestled under the see saw kicked in the face on the slide. I
don't care. don't cry tough it out no dolls god forbid no Lamb
Chop but plastic characters whose names end in thron and
mutant ninja transformers. I don't care. high fives slaps on the
back never an embrace do I care. no. army boot camp be all you
can be not who you want to be. I don't care. my dog would have
lived a simple dog life and I after forty-one years would be
writing about the mockingbird mimicking a squirrel to scare
the neighbor's cat or about medical supplies blockaded from
entering Gaza. do I care if his father left town his uncle pulled
him into the woods. no. what is beaten out of the boy what is
forced into the beaten-down boy so what. I don't care

my hapless dog would be dead today no matter how I work this
through if I do

he opened wide the window's slit crouched and climbed in.
I slept through the rattling unoiled half-broken sash cord
rollers I slept through his steps on the floor. a moon was
somewhere and somewhere was rain

blood on my shirt from my mouth never washed out. do I care
where he came from. no. I don't care

he had a mother he did. he he he had a mother. she caressed
him at least once he knew a caress. do I care. no. I don't care

why now a friend asks

I say to sleep

find the me back then

and like a chalk-covered schoolgirl
spell over and over

her name

write once and for all
my

over and over until swelled it explodes

our
splatters the walls—

I say

get this over with
and sleep

no name on a file card in the dusty basement the police
department records woman tells me she searched

disappeared names she calls them victim names fallen behind
metal cabinet drawers. stuck to the back of another 3x5. half-
names coffee stained or moisture smeared. disfigured names
Bs become Rs and Qs become Os. I'd sent ten dollars for the
41-year-old paper police report's hasty block capital letters in
Bic ink

and waited weeks for the manila envelope to slide through the
mailslot plunk on the floor. *maybe today I'll hear from St. Louis.*
my fingers would nibble the flap's sealed-tight corner and tear
open the top. a single page all I needed. name, address, date
above the scribbled blow-by-blow and a checked-off yes/no yes/
no column. subject object. subject object. signature shaky but
legible

nothing speaks nothing nowhere hides nowhere no shorter
longs to be no longer. take my word. the corner cigar store with
the case of ice cold Yoo-hoo at the cash register became a mall.
the neighbor's lackadaisical talk-over-it fence is now tall and
cement laced with furled-like-a-flag barbed wire

once on the brick stoop I'd sit with a sketchpad sit with the
Post Dispatch sit with Willa Cather and *O, Pioneers!* now I dig
through rubble for a buried cracked mirror. I dig for the lost
kernel of me dig and find at the mouth of a dried-out well a
single battered bucket with a rusted handle

skin I can't live in has a narrow door mouth and swollen window
eyes. parched adobe walls and a cracked pinched floor. despite
the invader intruder occupying force this skin I must reenter.
my pounding palms bleed rubies. knuckles hurt beyond sore.
the inaudible doorbell buzz stings like laughter

despite the invader intruder occupying force no one is home to
let me in. I climb through a hole in the roof

.

in skin I can't live in tattered wallpaper of pinto-riding cowboys
and rose-colored *fleurs-de-lis*. crumbled bathtub grout. broken
kitchen tiles in the sink. maple floorboards gouged by a wild
rhino's tusk

.

skin I can't live in once a dozen times a day I'd enter or leave.
door inside door pore inside pore. delinquent clutter hardened
grime seatless straightbacked chairs. the ceiling leaks the
cellar seeps what of repairs and mending. I am landlord
to myself. hammers pliers shingles lathe plaster rolls of
insulation—the storage pile is missing

refugee a coil unsprung

a *from* not a *to.* destinationless. I was a *from*

it was the oldest idea. home. it was one idea

turtle's eave and rafter. snail's cone roof. half-hidden
portable flesh

weight hauled on a muscled back

necessities tightly packed

what is necessity. a creased photo. a sister's palm-rubbed
rock

weigh each object. do you need the souvenir. the extra ounce
of intention in its cellophane wrap

weigh each objective

home is the range of one's instincts

senses on alert. breakfast sausage through the neighbor's
daisy-flowered kitchen curtains half parted. hot coffee steam

sparkling clean the faucet and knobs on her bathroom sink.
her home is pink and blue evening shadows. no skeins of lint
and loose thread on linoleum. her ring-eyed cat putters under
the stoop. her chattering schoolkids' Snickers wrappers fall
idly from their hands. home is luck aplenty, noise and sound
inviting as a crisp tidied-up bed

does she know on one day in one place pieces scatter. their
magnet poles never reengage

home is the range of one's instincts. light taps your eyelids your
eyes spring open to the dark

a window creak a tiny squeak the tentatively hung drapes open

just sleep sleep sleep. nothing worse can happen. the
unexpected's expected

because here is a bell to ring ring it. a clean fluffed pillow sink
your sleep into it. a blue shirt wear it don't go to bed naked with
wet hair

if "I am you back then" means we are not separate I am you
back then. take me

because here is your radio turn it on. AM FM short-wave.
because here is your rinsed clean Star Trek mug fill it and drink

roam the range of one's instincts

home

color size heat. distance proximity measure

a decades-long arm reaches across a table of crumbs
for what little remains of the loaf

a clipped yellow toenail sticks to the rim of the tub

rain screams like a jackhammer

the police siren bites a boy like a hound

innocence loses voice to sedition

home is the range of no feeling. instinctual as that is

home leans into distortion

home is slippery truth

home is *specious*

home is the coat that can't keep me warm or dry
buttons and holes I can't align

home yanks and pulls on its shortened leash
to always feel restraint

materials for the return gathered and saved

materials example: wool cotton and a yellow synthetic that simulates nylon. wicks off the sweat. holds the self-generated heat if there is heat in the bones of a young woman frozen in the crevice of a moment that does not melt

materials: glue for the gluing and odds-and-ends mosaic pieces to be glued. I glue the irregular-edged pieces like a madwoman quickly before the image shifts quickly before the adhesive dries

materials: time in a jar saved and stored and growing stale

materials donated with pseudo-generosity. try this try that. worked for me will work for you

sometimes the story is reconstructed in cardboard. sometimes moldy sugarcubes left over from imaginary tea. sometimes narrow switchbacks behind a green mountain lead me down a shy cenote's ladder into a limestone hole

materials for the story smell like the t-shirt forgotten under the bed, the heel- and toe-worn socks that missed the rim of the hamper, the underpants stuffed into the last square inch of the daisy-flower drawstring bag you take to the laundry where quarters stick in the slot. materials reek is what I'm saying reeked then and reek still after years of scouring with a brand-name liquid bleach materials for this story freeze in winter alleys

drown like telegraph lines under a pastel coral reef

float in the wind that winds your hair

dangle in Central Hardware on old pegboard hooks

squeeze tight against you in subway turnstiles

cram the last inch of elevator stinking sweat and out of breath

arrive cracked or water stained

stutter indecipherable words in the simplest language

materials are in the single-eye babies born in Fallujah
in their depleted uranium blood

materials are in the motherless sisterless fatherless brotherless
aunt- uncle- neighborless son- daughterless grandparentless
ghosts of evaporated towns

the rat-a-tat-tat clicking locks on windows and doors

the walls of prison. the walls of open-air prison

the nasal snoring sleep that is never and can never be a let-go
relaxed and confident sleep

materials are shovels to find and claim the names buried
under angled light buried between blades of heat. materials
are the pick-axes shivering overuse

materials are every woman and everywoman

a fist is raised. a roar is born a rumble in the distance

material is the eclipsed sun behind a sudden drone

look at aggression's lustful desire

find materials for this story in power fed with stolen land
uprooted trees suffocated springs

materials for this story haunt the margins. pores of skin.
molecules of metal. crack of stone

go to her wherever she is. on the rocky ridgeline with the view in all directions. on the tarpaper roof feeding pigeons cooped in their cage. find her above the sun spread like desolate roses on the snow. find her where the sun shirks behind stone and brick before pigeons set out on their missions after they have flown home

go to her though she doesn't call ask beg or hint. go to her she doesn't know she is waiting

bring her a siren bring her a bell bullhorn megaphone microphone but know she will choose to whisper. read the verbs on her lips the spittleless nouns

it's your hankering to talk don't twist her arm. with a running start jump over time's chasm and land on her side intact, pockets stuffed with the fractured present. remedial for you not for her

go to the place she calls home. find her hair permed or dyed. waist wider or trimmer. wrinkles gnawing at her cheeks. she'll answer to the very same name in a recognizable let-go laugh—ha! yes it's me you found, now leave

you don't leave

she'll need bandages or a tourniquet to tamp down the reopened wound. your dimestore first-aid kit too meager

whereabouts you find her is the accurately imprecise catch-all catch-nothing place. whereabouts when the young woman's eyes *my* eyes sprang open. whereabouts when the barking stopped and she I could hear the whispers between lines whispered numbers stories could hear stories. women men who did or didn't could or couldn't had or hadn't were or weren't able to find and flag the landmines. who hopscotched on narrow landmined streets in wide curbless landmined fears. you—connect the metal cluster dots time travel to her whereabouts. pinpoint the pivotal pause in the suspended calendar moment the single eye-opener if there was one. set a narrow tombstone where her small seat in the bleachers shifted

a narrow flat gray tombstone

watch the world come and go from the third row in the prefab metal bleachers erected for the first game dismantled for the second

and so on

the date on the tombstone is rubbed away. time is acquisition. sound is old slate

go to her where alone she waited for no one. skin burns to be touched. shoulders to be cradled. thoughts are growing thistle

in *whereabouts* "one in every" grows eyes in the back of her head or if that is impossible twists her neck 180

I bring her a map. at worst she'll shine her shoes with the stripmined flattened hills. the redlined city blocks. she'll wrap the fish. she'll shelve a hemisphere or a township or a subway line for later

in our unzipped suitcases shirts skirts deodorant scarves sandals not so different. the identical hair-pick comb

we're meeting because

I ask

time travelers we meet at gravity's edge where the likely
and unexpected take cover. trade dog-eared marked-up
annotated maps

a washed-out alley. a school collapsed. a library set on fire.
she'll show me around until the rain subsides and the wind is
weighted clay

blindfolded pointing left right with one finger

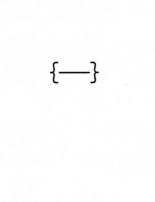

how long I thrashed in the deep recess between tic and toc
where bedfellows *never* and *forever* entwine. where loud and
silent nothing and everything cower

walls of spiked metal. walls of leper sores. every breath threw
me like a ragdoll against the walls

and sound louder than inner earth swallowing a fault louder
than a sonic boom louder than his *don't move* rasp his *or I'll
kill you* whisper the thunder of his knife on my chin blood
rattling my engine heart

the pause filled quickly with instant-cement powder-ground
bones

a squirrel somewhere squawked like a hen never mind. lovers
fought then wailed in sex. babies cried. an ordinary night

meanwhile the pause's bodysuit stretched over time's
massive rump. slipped up time's thunder thighs into its
crotch into time's moist and itching crotch

all and nothing coalesced. a gel

forget containment confinement. the pause hobbles. its bent
hobo stick about to snap from the unwieldy bag of bones. bones
on the border nettled with Arizona cactus thorns. bones in
an alley pierced with hypodermic needles. bones of a famine
bones of a sanction bones of blockaded antibiotics bones of
withheld vaccine. bones of the Disappeared. bones weak as the
poles of a refugee tent. bones sunk in contaminated water and
bones of the billion women hauling pounds of water in pots on
their heads miles every day skulls crushed by the weight

I thought I was nothing after nothing was left then tripped on the miniscule kernel that was left of me

it resembled a paralyzed speck

paralyzed eyes, leaden feet, hands tied, mind in mud

paralysis that began with obedience to paralysis. his three hands one crushing my mouth one holding a knife at my throat one whose flashlight seared my eyes *don't move* I lay there

unmoving I lay there unfleeing I wasn't there. I was. I wasn't. I was outside me I was inside me

I was there but nowhere to be found

the deflated dehydrated minute pause reinflates rehydrates. is there room in a room for eternity swelled like a sponge

eternity scattered in all directions and stuck in one place

eternity is the trick of the trade

empty bottles line my window sill. piano wire crisscrosses my window frame. lights in every room. list of numbers taped to the phone the phone a handreach away

some people sleep with a baseball bat on the mattress some with a knife near the pillow. I say don't sleep when you sleep sleep sitting up in a chair

I say tell every lover you scream in your sleep they mustn't touch you when you scream in your sleep

before I knew before fear assured me I won't drown in airless
non-time, the dog

how long in the sealed coffin vibrating from shovelfuls of dirt
before the dog dug me up furiously like a just-remembered
bone. how long in the underground tunnel the entry/exit
collapsed before it howled my release

how long in the far-flung bottom of the well I had just fallen
in not even chasing a coin just fallen in just happened to be
there and failed to not fall in

but for the dog

Acknowledgements

Grateful acknowledgement to the *Beloit Poetry Journal* for publishing the poem on page 25 (titled "He Opened the Window's Slit and Climbed In").

"Home is the range of one's instincts" is a quote from Terry Tempest Williams, *An Unspoken Hunger.*

Denise Bergman is the author of three books of poetry. *A Woman in Pieces Crossed a Sea* explores the Statue of Liberty as it sat disassembled for one year in New York Harbor. *The Telling* is a book-length poem generated by a relative's one-sentence secret: she believed that as a child refugee she had accidentally killed her mother. *Seeing Annie Sullivan,* based on the early life of Helen Keller's teacher, was translated into Braille. Denise edited the anthology of urban poetry *City River of Voices.* She lives in Massachusetts.